What the Romans did for us

Alison Hawes

Published 2009 by
A & C Black Publishers Ltd.
36 Soho Square, London, W1D 3QY
www.acblack.com

ISBN HB 978-1-4081-0858-1
PB 978-1-4081-1286-1

Series consultant: Gill Matthews
Text copyright © 2009 Alison Hawes

This book is produced using paper that is made from wood grown in managed, sustainable forests. It is natural, renewable and recyclable. The logging and manufacturing processes conform to the environmental regulations of the country of origin.

Produced for A & C Black by Calcium.
Printed and bound in China by C&C Offset Printing Co.

All the internet addresses given in this book were correct at the time of going to press. The author and publishers regret any inconvenience caused if addresses have changed or sites have ceased to exist, but can accept no responsibility for any such changes.

Acknowledgements
The author would like to thank Mr J. Brinded for his invaluable help and advice whilst researching this title.

The publishers would like to thank the following for their kind permission to reproduce their photographs:
Cover: Shutterstock: Malibu Books, Elena Elisseeva, Kate Linesz, Jasenka Luksa.
Pages: Bridgeman Art Library: Museo e Gallerie Nazionali di Capodimonte, Naples, Italy, Lauros/Giraudon 6; Dreamstime: Rafael Laguillo 4, Kati Neudert 14b; Shutterstock: Chad Bontrager 15b, Joseph Calev 16-17, Franck Camhi 21, Jacek Chabraszewski 9b, Anna Dzondzua 10, Elena Elisseeva 14-15, Liv Friis-Larsen 9tcl, Joe Gough 19, Laurence Gough 18, Chris Green 12, George Green 13, Margo Harrison 9tl, Hauhu 17b, Tomo Jesenicnik 9tr, Verity Johnson 8, Jasenka Luksa 20, Zaichenko Olga 11bl, Losevsky Pavel 11t, PhotoCreate 7, Tatiana Popova 16bl, Rainbow 5, Jack Scrivener 11bc, Radovan Spurny 9tcr, Margaret M Stewart 11br, Ultimathule 16br.

Contents

The Romans and Celts 4

Language 6

Food 8

Roads 10

Towns 12

Baths 14

Toilets 16

Homes 18

Numbers 20

Glossary 22

Further Information 23

Index 24

The Romans and Celts

The Romans came from Rome, Italy. They had a big, strong army that **conquered** lots of countries. The Romans built a mighty empire.

Roman invasion

About 2,000 years ago, the Romans conquered England, Wales, and parts of Scotland. People called the Celts lived in Britain when the Romans **invaded**. The Romans **ruled** the Celts for 400 years.

The Roman Empire was ruled by an emperor. This is a statue of Emperor Nero.

The Romans and the Celts were very different people. They:

- [ ] wore different clothes
- [ ] spoke different languages
- [ ] ate different foods
- [ ] lived in different houses
- [ ] had different ideas about how to live

When the Romans came, they brought their different ways with them.

The Celts lived in simple, wooden houses, like this one. Roman houses were larger and made of stone or brick.

Language

The Romans did not speak the same language as the Celts. The Romans spoke a language called Latin. When the Romans conquered Britain, some Celts also learned to speak Latin.

A Roman girl learning to read and write.

Latin today

Today, many languages in the world use words that come from Latin. Many children also have Latin names. ....

DO YOU HAVE A LATIN NAME?

Amanda Dominic Mica
Anthony Stacy

Teaching the Celts

The Celts did not read or write before the Romans came. The Romans taught rich and important Celts to read and write in Latin.

A B C D E F G H I

Our alphabet (top) is like the Roman alphabet (bottom).

The word "library" comes from the Latin word liber, which means "book".

Food

The Celts were farmers. They kept animals for food, wool, and leather. They grew food such as wheat, peas, and beans. They cooked food on a fire on the floor of their house.

Roman diet

The Romans ate different food from the Celts. Many of the foods we eat today were first brought to Britain by the Romans.

Roman plates and spoons

The Romans did not eat with knives and forks. They used their fingers and a spoon.

DID YOU KNOW?

These foods were not eaten in Britain until the Romans came.

Apples **Cherries** **Chicken** **Pears**

Take-away meal

Some Romans bought hot food from shops and bars. This was a new idea to the Celts. Today, we sometimes buy take-away food, just like the Romans did.

Many Romans ate burgers, just like we do today.

Make a Roman burger

1. Mix minced beef with pine nuts, salt, and stock.

2. Make into round shapes and fry until cooked.

Roads

When the Romans came to Britain, the soldiers built 16,000 km (10,000 miles) of roads. They wanted straight roads so the army could travel quickly from place to place.

Most Roman roads were very straight.

Built to last

Roman roads were well made. They lasted for hundreds of years. Many of the roads we use today are built on top of old Roman roads.

HAVE YOU TRAVELLED ON A ROMAN ROAD?

Ermine Street Dere Street
Watling Street Fosse Way

Modern roads are measured in miles. Roman roads were, too!

Trade roads

Good roads made it easier for the Celts to travel and **trade** with the Romans.

The Celts sold many things to the Romans.

Wheat   **Hunting dogs**   **Silver**

Towns

Before the Romans invaded, the Celts lived in farms and villages. The Romans were used to living in towns with shops and markets. They built many towns in Britain.

Built to plan

Most Roman towns were built to the same plan. A big square, called a **forum**, was built in the middle of the town. Walls were built around the town.

The Romans introduced shops to Britain.

A town below!

Many of the towns we live in today are built on top of towns that were first built by the Romans.

The city of York was built by the Romans.

DO YOU LIVE IN A ROMAN TOWN?

Bath   London   St. Albans   York

Towns with names ending in -caster, -chester, or -cester were also built by the Romans.

Baths

The Romans liked to keep clean. So they built public baths in many towns. This was a new idea.

DID YOU KNOW?

The Romans also kept their teeth clean just like we do today. The Romans brushed their teeth with a powder made of bone or eggshells!

Transporting water

The Romans made sure towns had clean, fresh water. They dug wells and built **aqueducts** to bring clean water from the hills to the towns.

Aqueducts were made of stone.

The city of Bath is named after the baths the Romans built there.

Keeping clean

The Romans did not have soap. They put oil on their skin, instead. A slave took the oil and the dirt off with a scraper.

ROMAN BATHS
HAD MANY ROOMS:

Some were very hot
Some were very cold
Some were just warm

Toilets

The Romans built public toilets in Britain. This was a new idea. Rich Romans also built toilets in their own homes.

No privacy!

Roman toilets did not have doors. They were not private. People sat next to each other and could chat to their friends if they wanted!

DID YOU KNOW?

The Romans did not use toilet paper. Instead they used a sponge on a stick.

Clean toilets

Some Roman toilets had water running underneath them to keep them clean. Sewer pipes took the dirty water away.

WC

WC

Some Roman toilets were ·········· free, and in some you had to pay – just like like public toilets used today.

Homes

The Celts lived in round houses made from wood or stone. They had just one room and a roof of straw or turf.

Roman houses

Roman houses were a different shape. Some had many rooms. Sometimes they had more than one **storey**.

Town or country?

Rich Romans built homes called villas in the countryside. Some rich Celts also built villas in the countryside.

Rich Romans decorated their homes with mosaics.

DID YOU KNOW?

Hot air from a fire under the floors heated some Roman houses. This was an early form of central heating.

Houses today

Many homes today are built using the same materials that the Romans used, such as concrete and glass.

WHAT IS YOUR HOUSE BUILT OF?

Concrete glass bricks wood

Most houses today have many rooms, and most have central heating.

Numbers

The Romans used seven letters to write their numerals. Some numbers were very long. The number 738 looked like this: DCCXXXVIII.

Letter	Number
I	1
V	5
X	10
L	50
C	100
D	500
M	1,000

Most people now use Arabic numbers, but Roman numbers are still kept for certain uses.

Many of the clocks and watches we use today have Roman numerals.

Counting people

The Romans counted the number of people who lived in their empire. They called this a **census**. We still have a census in Britain today. It happens every ten years.

Roman calendar

The Romans also gave us our calendar. So, like the Romans, we have seven days in a week, 365 days in a year and 366 days in a **leap year**.

Glossary

aqueduct a pipe or channel for carrying water

census a count of the number of people living in one place

conquer to overcome an enemy

forum a Roman market square with shops and public buildings

invade to attack another country with an army

leap year a year, once every four years, that has an extra day

mosaic a picture made from tiny pieces of stone or glass

rule to be in charge of

storey a level of a building that is above its ground floor

trade to buy and sell goods

Further Information

Websites

The Roman Empire children's website at:
www.roman-empire.net/children/achieve.html

The BBC Romans website at:
www.bbc.co.uk/schools/romans/invasion.shtml

Find out more about the Celts at:
www.bbc.co.uk/wales/celts/index.shtml

Places to visit

Bignor Roman Villa
Bignor
West Sussex

Brading Roman Villa
Isle of Wight

Museum of London
London Wall
London

Roman Baths
Bath
Avon

Welwyn Roman Baths
Welwyn
Herts

**Aldborough Roman Town
and Museum**
Aldborough
North Yorks

Buster Ancient Farm
Near Chalton
Hampshire

Verulanium Museum
St. Albans
Hertfordshire

Index

alphabet 7
aqueducts 14, 15
army 4, 10

baths 14–15

calendar 21
Celts 4, 5, 6, 7, 8, 9, 11
census 20
conquered 4, 6
cooking 8

emperors 4, 21
empire 4, 20

farmers 8
food 8–9
forum 12

gods 21

heating 19
houses 5, 18–19

invasion 4, 12

language 6
Latin 6
leap year 21

miles 11
mosaics 18

numbers 20–21

public toilets 16

reading 7
roads 10–11

sewer 17
shops 12
slave 15
storeys 18

take-away food 9
toilets 16–17
towns 12–13
trade 11

villas 18

walls 12, 13
washing 14–15
water 14, 17
wells 14
writing 7